FINITE ELEMENT METHODS

IMPORTANT 2 MARKS QUESTIONS & ANSWERS

A.JOHN PRESIN KUMAR

M.RAJESH

A.SIVASANKAR

Made with ♥ on the Notion Press Platform
www.notionpress.com

This Book is dedicated to the ALMIGHTY for all the blessings showered...!!!

Contents

Foreword

The main purpose of this book to provide the readers, especially the students community with enriched knowledge on the 2 marks questions and answers of Finite Element Methods. This FEM subject normally appears in the seventh semester of B.E or B.Tech (Mechanical Engineering) course. Students will definitely find this small book very useful not only for their academic studies but also for their job and placement opportunities, where nowadays lots of technical questions are expected from problem oriented subjects like Finite Element Methods.

Most of the companies especially in the core Mech/Auto category are mainly focussing on Design oriented subject knowledge from the students.

Have a good reading...

Preface

Students community are always in need of a good guide especially for their preparation towards competitive exams. Enriched knowledge on the 2 marks questions and answers of Finite Element Methods in this case is an added benefit to them. Students will find this book as a very useful guide not for facing their job and placement opportunities...

All the very best...!!!

Acknowledgements

We thank Dr.P.Vijayabalan, Head of the Department of Mechanical Engineering, Hindustan Institute of Technology & Science, Kelambakkam, Chennai-603103. Tamilnadu, India. for all the helps he provided during the preparation of this book.

Prologue

A grand success for students in the Job and placement opportunities clearly lies in a thorough preparation on the basic concepts of problematic subjects like FEM, where nowadays lots of technical questions are expected from this. Most of the companies especially in the core Aero/Mech/Mechatronics/Auto category are mainly focussing on the Theory and also the Design oriented subject knowledge from the students. Books such as this, serves that purpose very well.

CHAPTER ONE

FINITE ELEMENT METHODS 2 MARKS QUESTIONS & ANSWERS UNIT 1 INTRODUCTION

Define FEA.

Finite element method (FEM) is a popular method for numerically solving differential equations arising in engineering and mathematical modeling.

Mention any one software related to FEA.

ANSYS

List out any four advantages of finite element method.

The Advantages of the Finite Element Method

- Modeling. FEM allows for easier modeling of complex geometrical and irregular shapes. ...
- Adaptability. ...
- Accuracy. ...
- Time-dependent simulation. ...
- Boundaries. ...
- Visualization.

Restate the reason why polynomial type interpolation functions are mostly used in FEM.

It is easier to formulate and computerize the finite element equations with polynomial- type interpolation functions. Specifically, it is easier to perform differentiation or integration with polynomials.

Mention the advantages of Rayleigh Ritz method.

The Rayleigh Ritz method is a significant concept in the field of Engineering. This proven approach is mostly used for finding approximate solutions to various boundary value problems. It employs the principles of calculus of variations to compute approximated values.

Differentiate the Ritz technique from the nodal approximation method.

Ritz method assumes trial functions.

And these trial functions must satisfy boundary conditions over the entire structure.

State how is it possible to develop the equilibrium equation for a finite element.

First it is needed to split the entire structure into its component parts and then derive the force *equilibrium equations using the assemblage of element wise equations.*

<u>Restate constitutive law</u>**.**

This constitutive law enforces compatibility through the use of a "penalty" stress that is proportional to the violation of compatibility.

<u>**List the various methods of solving boundary value problems.**</u>

Analytical methods.

Numerical methods.

<u>Illustrate how to formulate the boundary conditions in FEM.</u>

By following some assumptions, the boundary conditions are formed.

They are

The body forces, if any exist, cannot vary in the thickness direction and cannot have components in the z direction; the applied boundary forces must be uniformly distributed across the thickness (i.e. constant in the z direction); and no loads can be applied on the parallel planes bounding to the bottom surfaces.

<u>Differentiate between primary and secondary variables.</u>

Primary variables are original and more detailed with specific nature whereas the secondary variables are not.

<u>Recall the way of identifying types of EigenValue Problems.</u>

"Eigenvalue" means characteristic value. These types of problems show up in many areas involving boundary-value problems, where we may not be able to obtain an analytical solution

Mention the weak formulation of FEA.

The weak formulation turns a differential equation into an integral equation. Integration by parts reduces the order of differentiation to provide numerical advantages, and generates natural boundary conditions for specifying fluxes at the boundaries.

Distinguish between Error and Residual.

The error of an observation is the deviation of the observed value from the true value of a quantity of interest (for example, a population mean). The residual is the difference between the observed value and the estimated value of the quantity of interest (for example, a sample mean).

Discuss Ritz method.

Ritz method converts the differential equation of a boundary value problem into a set of algebraic equations using the corresponding integral form.

Recall the way of developing total potential energy of a structural system

The total potential energy of the system is the sum of the potential energies of all the types.

In order to get the total potential, it is needed to consider addition of all its constituent elements.

State the principle of minimum potential energy.

For conservative structural systems, of all the kinematically admissible deformations, those corresponding to the equilibrium state extremize (i.e., minimize or maximize) the total potential energy. If the extremum is a minimum, the equilibrium state is stable.

Differentiate between initial value problem and boundary value problem.

Typically, initial value problems involve time dependent functions and boundary value problems are spatial. So, with an initial value problem one knows how a system evolves in terms of the differential equation and the state of the system at some fixed time.

List out the advantages of finite element method over other numerical analysis method.

-

- Modeling. FEM allows for easier modeling of complex geometrical and irregular shapes. ...
- Adaptability. ...
- Accuracy. ...
- Time-dependent simulation. ...
- Boundaries. ...
- Visualization.

List the various weighted residual methods.

Collocation *Method* ·

Subdomain *Method* ·

Galerkin *Method* ·

Least Squares *Method.*

Mention the methods generally associated with the finite element analysis.

The following two methods are generally associated with the finite element analysis. They are1)Force method. 2)Displacement or stiffness method.

Summarize the meaning of the term Discretization.

Discretization in the finite element method (FEM) refers to the process of breaking down a continuous domain (such as a physical object or a field) into a finite number of smaller, simpler parts called finite elements.

Mention types of elements.

*

- Triangle element.
- Quadrangle element.
- Tetrahedron element.
- Hexahedron element.
- Pentahedron element (prism)

Siffness method involves finding ______ as unknown parameter.

Ans: Displacement

Restate the meaning of Degrees of Freedom.

Degrees of freedom are the *number of independent variables that can be estimated in a statistical analysis.*

List any two FEA softwares.

SimScale

ANSYS

Define the term node.

Adjacent elements are connected to each other AT the nodes. A node is simply a point in space, defined by its coordinates, at which DEGREES OF FREEDOM are defined.

CHAPTER TWO

UNIT 2 ONE-DIMENSIONAL PROBLEMS

Write about 1D heat transfer through a fin.

Heat transfer through fins is a process that involves the transfer of heat from a hotter surface to a cooler one through a finned surface

Define shape function.

The shape function is a function that helps interpolate variable values in between two different nodes with discrete values of the variable.

Mention the shape function of a two node line element

$\theta(x) = [N1,x\ N2,x\ N3,x\ N4,x]\{w1\ \theta1\ w2\ \theta2\}T$.

List out the important stiffness matrix properties.

The properties of the stiffness matrix are

- It is a symmetric matrix.
- The sum of elements in any column must be equal to zero.
- It is an unstable element therefore the determinant is equal to zero.
- The joint displacements are treated as basic unknowns.

Mention the characteristics of shape functions.

Properties of Shape Functions

- At a node, the value of shape function is either 0 or 1.
- Summation of all the shape functions at any point is equal to 1.
- Continuity. Within the element boundary, the polynomial approximation for u is $C\infty$ continuous. ...
- Completeness.

Differentiate global and local coordinate.

The global coordinate system defines the position and translation of a body in space. Local coordinate systems define how limbs and body segments articulate about joints.

Define global FEM.

A global-local finite element analysis procedure is developed based on the fast convergent nature of FEM in displacement.

Define natural coordinate system

A natural coordinate system is a local coordinate system that permits the specification of any point inside the element by a set of nondimensional numbers whose magnitude lies between 0 and 1.

Restate the meaning for quadratic bar element.

The quadratic bar element is *a one-dimensional finite element* where the local and global coordinates coincide.

List the types of dynamic analysis problems.

- Real eigenvalue analysis (undamped free vibrations).

- Linear frequency response analysis (steady-state response of linear structures to loads that vary as a function of frequency).
- Linear transient response analysis (response of linear structures to loads that vary as a function of time).

Define mode superposition technique.

Modal superposition is a powerful idea of obtaining solutions. It is applicable to both free vibration and forced vibration problems. The basic idea. To use free vibrations mode shapes to uncouple equations of motion. The uncoupled equations are in terms of new variables called the modal coordinates.

Define mass matrix for a 1D linear bar element.

The element mass matrix of the faces and the core, decomposed into an inertia terms of translation in x, y and z directions and rotation around x and y as well as coupling terms of translation–rotation.

Recall what is transverse vibration of beam.

Transverse vibration in beams is a significant mode of vibration in a continuous system. - There are four main beam theories: Euler Bernoulli, Release, Shear, and Timoshenko, each with its assumptions and applications.

Recall one-dimensional dynamic structural analysis problems.

Dynamic analysis is a simple extension of static analysis. In addition, all real structures potentially have an infinite number of displacements.

Write about boundary conditions.

Boundary conditions are constraints necessary for the solution of a boundary value problem. A boundary value problem is a differential equation (or system of differential equations) to be solved in a domain on whose boundary a set of conditions is known.

Define the transverse vibration.

A vibration in which the element moves to and fro in a direction perpendicular to the direction of the advance of the wave.

Mention the meaning of spring system in FEM.

A spring system can be thought of as the simplest case of the finite element method for solving problems in statics.

Explain the way the global stiffness matrix differs from element stiffness matrix.

For a more complex spring system, a 'global' stiffness matrix is required – i.e. one that describes the behaviour of the complete system, and not just the individual springs.

Define longitudinal vibration of the bar element.

This means that the *particles of the bar move in the direction parallel to the axis of the bar*

CHAPTER THREE

UNIT 3 TWO DIMENSIONAL CONTINUUM

Define displacement function.

The displacement function is defined as the function that describes the displacement within the element in terms of the nodal values of the element.

Define a two-dimensional FEM problem.

Two dimensional elements are defined by three or more nodes in a two dimensional. plane (i.e., x, y plane).

List out the application of two-dimensional problems.

Composite laminates.

Automobile body parts.

Recall steady state heat transfer.

In the realm of heat transfer, a system is said to be in a steady state when the temperature and heat transfer rate within it do not change with time.

Define two-dimensional scalar variable problem.

In Two dimensional scalar variable problems, elements are defined by three or more nodes in two dimensional plane (i x and y. plane).

Restate the meaning of FEA.

Finite Element Analysis.

This is the process of <u>simulating</u> the behavior of an object or assemblage of objects when it's exposed to specified physical conditions, which can be stable or varying.

Define QST(Quadratic strain Triangle) element.

Six noded triangular element is known as Linear Strain Triangle (LST) or as. Quadratic Displacement Triangle. Ten noded triangular elements are known as. Quadratic Strain Triangles (QST) or Cubic Displacement Triangles.

Relate pathline with streamline.

Streamlines, streaklines and pathlines are *field lines* in a fluid flow. They differ only when the flow changes with time, that is, when the flow is not steady.

Displacement in two dimensional element involves the notations _______ and _______ for x and y directions.

ANS: x and y

Define interpolation function.

Interpolation is a method of deriving a simple function from the given discrete data set such that the function passes through the provided data points.

Define the CST and LST elements.

- A CST element is a three noded linear triangular element having 2 nodes per side while an LST element is six noded quadratic triangular element having 3 nodes per side.

<u>**Distinguish between scalar and vector variable problems in 2D.**</u>

A scalar quantity has only magnitude, but no direction. Vector quantity has both magnitude and direction. Every scalar quantity is one-dimensional. Vector quantity can be one, two or three-dimensional.

<u>Define</u> **stiffness matrix.**

In the finite element method for the numerical solution of elliptic partial differential equations, the stiffness matrix is a matrix that represents the system of linear equations that must be solved in order to ascertain an approximate solution to the differential equation.

<u>Give</u> **the abbreviation for LST.**

Linear Strain Triangular

<u>Restate the meaning of area coordinates</u>.

An *area coordinate*, x , is *defined* as the ratio of the *area* of a subtriangle to the total *area* of the element.

<u>Define Isoparametric elements with suitable examples.</u>

The term isoparametric is derived from the use of the same shape functions (or interpolation functions) [N] to define the element's geometric shape as are used to define the displacements within the element.

Recall four node quadrilateral elements.

Four Node Quadrilateral elements are a four-node plane-strain element using bilinear isoparametric formulation.

Define geometric Isotropy.

Geometric isotropy or invariance in finite element modeling, means the displacement shapes of an element do not change with a change in the local coordinate system.2

Restate Lagrange shape function.

The *shape function* is a function that helps interpolate variable values in between two different nodes with discrete values of the variable.

CHAPTER FOUR

UNIT 4 AXISYMMETRIC CONTINUUM

Recall the meaning of aisymmetric.

Axisymmetric elements are triangular tori such that each element is symmetric with respect to geometry and loading about an axis such as the z axis.

<u>Classify the types of shell element.</u>

Quadrilateral thin shell element (S8R5), Quadrilateral thin shell element (S4R5) and Triangular thin shell element (STRI65).

<u>Define 2D vector variable problems</u>

In vector variable problems, *All boundary conditions must be symmetric about the axis of revolution.* • All loading conditions must be symmetric about the axis of revolution.

Restate the meaning of elasticity equations.

Hooke's law, F = kx, where the applied force F equals a constant k times the displacement or change in length x. elasticity, ability of a deformed material body to return to its original shape and size when the forces causing the deformation are removed. Such equations are called elasticity equations.

Define plane stress and plane strain.

In continuum mechanics, a material is said to be under *plane stress if the stress vector is zero across a particular plane.*

Plane strain is a two-dimensional state of strain in which all the shape changes of a material happen on a single plane.

Discuss 'Principal stresses".

Principal stress represents the maximum and minimum normal stresses that occur within a material when subjected to complex loading conditions.

Restate linear triangular elements.

A linear triangular element is a two-dimensional finite element that has three nodes and three sides shown in Fig. 6.8. It has three vertices and the nodes have coordinates (x_1, y_1) , (x_2, y_2) , (x_3, y_3) in global Cartesian coordinate system.

Define bilinear quadrilateral elements.

a type of element used in finite element analysis which is used to approximate in a 2D domain the exact solution to a given differential equation.

Write the meaning of solid mechanics.

Solid mechanics, as a branch of continuum mechanics, is the study of the deformation or motion of solids under external applied loadings including forces, displacements, temperature changes, or other agents.

Distinguish between plate and shell elements.

Plates are flat surfaces applied with lateral loading, with bending behaviors dominating the structural response. Shells are structures which span over curved surfaces; they carry both membrane and bending forces under lateral loading.

Define axisymmetric formulation.

In order to formulate 2D axisymmetric elements, we shall define the displacement field by two components in the r–z plane: u for displacement in the r or radial direction; and w for displacement in the z or axial direction.

Define nodal points in axisymmetric triangular elements.

The nodal points of an axisymmetric triangular element describe circumferential lines. In plane stress problems, stresses exist only in the x-y plane.

Write about axisymmetric solid elements.

Axisymmetric solid elements are 3D *elements* that are used to *model* metal structures that have *axisymmetric* geometry.

Define cylindrical coordinates system.

A cylindrical coordinate system is a three-dimensional coordinate system that *specifies point positions by the distance from a chosen reference axis.*

Mention the meaning of polar coordinates.

When each point on a plane of a two-dimensional coordinate system is decided by a distance from a reference point and an angle is taken from a reference direction, it is known as the polar coordinate system.

Recall the type of strains developed in aisymmetric problems.

In axisymmetric problems, the radial displacements develop circumferential strains that induce stresses σr , σθ , σz and τrz where r, θ, and z indicate the radial, circumferential, and longitudinal directions, respectively.

Assess the required conditions for a problem assumed to be axisymmetric.

Problem domain must be symmetric about the axis of revolution. All boundary conditions must be symmetric about the axis of revolution. All loading conditions must be symmetric about the axis of revolution.

Give example for a plane strain problem.

A typical example of plane strain is the pressurisation of long cylinders

Give example for a plane stress problem.

If a structure is loaded in a plane and the load is constant across the cross section, the problem can be treated as a plane-stress problem.

Give example for an aisymmetric element.

Cooling towers, submarine pressure hulls, offshore drilling rigs, aerosol cans, radomes, nuclear reactors, etc.

CHAPTER FIVE

UNIT 5 ISOPARAMETRIC FORMULATION

Illustrate the purpose of Isoparameteric element.

The purpose of the isoparametric formulation is to create shape functions that would ensure the compatibility of the displacement between neighboring elements while maintaining the requirements for shape functions

Differentiate between Isoparametric and sub- parametric elements.

If the same number of elements are used to defined geometry as well as displacement the element is called isoparametric elements. 2) The elements in which less number of nodes is used to defined geometry compare to the number of nodes used to defined displacement, the element is called sub parametric elements.

Define isoparametric formulation.

By means of isoparametric formulation, we can produce elements with curved and irregular boundaries. This is done by making use of a mapping from the physical space of the actual curved element into a natural coordinate space of a par- ent element with straight and regular boundaries

Explain the Jacobian transformation.

The Jacobian can be understood by considering a unit area in the new coordinate space; and examining how that unit area transforms when mapped into xy coordinate space in which the integral is visually understood.

Define super parametric element.

If the number of nodes used for defining the geometry is more than of nodes used for defining the displacement is known as super parametric element

Define Jacobian matrix.

The *Jacobian matrix* is an important component of the *isoparametric* element formulation. It is commonly denoted as [J] and represents a "scaling" factor.

List out the main advantage of Gauss quadrature numerical integration for Isoparametric element

One important advantage of Gaussian quadrature formulas is that the end points are not used in the integration. In many computations, end points have discontinuities, and therefore, using the functional values at the end points is not desirable.

Define Isoparametric element.

Isoparametric elements are a type of finite element used in numerical methods, particularly in finite element analysis (FEA). They are characterized by the fact that the same shape functions are used to interpolate both the geometry of the element and the field variables (such as displacement, temperature, etc.) within that element.

Discuss about Numerical integration.

Numerical integration is a method in which approximate solution of definite integral is evaluated using numerical techniques. In this method the polynomial function is evaluated at some known base points (sampling points) with weighting co-efficient.

Discuss about Gauss-quadrature method.

Gauss quadrature uses the function values evaluated at a number of interior points (hence it is an open quadrature rule) and corresponding weights to approximate the integral by a weighted sum.

Differentiate between implicitly and explicitly methods of numerical

Integration.

The explicit method is easier to program and can be calculated within a shorter time. But its stability is so low that you need to use a step size small enough to prevent divergence. On the contrary, the implicit method has high stability and converges if you set proper parameters.

Differentiate between geometric and material non-linearity.

Small deformation analysis based on geometric nonlinearity is required for some applications, like analysis involving cables, arches and shells. Material nonlinearity involves the nonlinear behavior of a material based on a current deformation, deformation history, rate of deformation, temperature, pressure, and so on.

List out the significance of Jacobian transformation

The significance of the Jacobian in integration lies in the fact that it ensures that the integral is evaluated over the same region of integration, regardless of the choice of variables. In other words, it allows for a change of variables in the integrand while preserving the value of the integral. This property makes the Jacobian a fundamental tool in many areas of mathematics and physics, where integrals are used to model physical phenomena and solve problems in a wide range of fields.

Define Isoparametric element with suitable examples.

The term isoparametric is derived from the use of the same shape functions (or interpolation functions) [N] to define the element's geometric shape as are used to define the displacements within the element. Ex: Bar elements

Recall standard displacement for four noded quadrilateral element.

The standard displacement field of a four-node quadrilateral element is bilinear. Therefore if we overlap two quadrilateral elements together, similar to the case with the three-node triangular elements

Write about the meaning of the term quadrilateral.

A quadrilateral is a polygon having four sides, four angles, and four vertices. The word 'quadrilateral' is derived from the Latin words 'quadri,' which means four, and 'latus', which means side.

Define quadrature method.

The process of determining the area of a plane geometric figure by dividing it into a collection of shapes of known area (mostly rectangles) and then finding the limit of the sum of these areas.

Distinguish between trapezoidal rule and Simpson's rule.

The two methods differ in the order of their basic functions, which is how they derive their names: The trapezoidal rule uses a piecewise linear interpolant (i.e., first-order polynomials), while Simpson's rule uses a quadratic interpolant (i.e., second-order polynomials).

Distinguish between trapezoidal rule and Gauss quadrature.

An open quadrature rule is when $f(x)$ is not evaluated at the endpoints. The Trapezoid Rule is a closed Quadrature rule where $f(x)$ is only evaluated at the endpoints a and b on the interval [a, b].

Define higher order element.

Higher order element: For any element if the interpolation polynomial is of order two or more the element is known as higher order element. In higher order element the field variable variation is non-linear. Also it may be a complex or multiplex element. In higher order element some secondary nodes are produced in addition to the primary nodes in order to match the number of nodal degrees of freedom with the number of polynomial coefficients in the polynomial interpolation.

****

(In addition to the above questions, students can prepare all the important formulae also like Stiffness matrix, Shape functions in all units. Thanks)

****

CHAPTER SIX

FEM – SYLLABUS (Just topics are given. Subjected to changes based on institution)

MODULE1:INTRODUCTION

Historical Background – Mathematical Modeling of field problems in Engineering –Governing Equations – Discrete and continuous models – Boundary, Initial and Eigen Value problems– Weighted Residual Methods – Variational Formulation of Boundary Value Problems – Ritz Technique – Basic concepts of the Finite Element Method.

SuggestedReadings: Application to bar element,Application to the continuum.

MODULE2:ONE DIMENSIONAL PROBLEMS

One DimensionalSecond Order Equations -Derivation of Shape functions and Stiffness matrices and force vectors-Galarkin approach - Assembly of stiffness matrix and load vector - Solution of problems from solid mechanics and heat transfer-Finite element equations - Longitudinal vibration frequencies and mode.

SuggestedReadings: Applications to plane trusses, Quadratic shape functions.

MODULE3: TWO DIMENSIONAL CONTINUUM

Introduction - Finite element modelling - Scalar valued problem - Poisson equation -Laplace equation - Triangular elements - Element stiffness matrix - Force vector -Galarkin approach - Temperature effects - stress strain relations – plane problems of elasticity – element equations – assembly – need for quadrature formulae –transformations to natural coordinates – Gaussian quadrature – example problems in plane stress, plane strain using MATLAB© and Abaqus.

SuggestedReadings: Structural mechanics applications.

MODULE4:AXISYMMETRIC CONTINUUM

Axisymmetric formulation - Element stiffness matrix and force vector - Galarkin approach - Body forces and temperature effects - Stress calculations - Boundary conditions - Applications to cylinders under internal or external pressures - Rotating discs - Plate and shell elements.

SuggestedReadings: Axisymmetric applications.

MODULE5:ISOPARAMETRIC FORMULATION

Natural co-ordinate systems – Isoparametric elements with mat lab coding – Shape functions for iso parametric elements – One and two dimensions– Numerical integration and application to plane stress problems - Matrix solution techniques –Solutions Techniques to Dynamic problems – Introduction to Analysis Software.

SuggestedReadings: Application of four node quadrilateral.

CHAPTER SEVEN

BOOKS

CKrishnamoorthy,(2017),FiniteElementAnalysis:TheoryandProgramming,McGrawHill Education;2ndedition.

AnandV.Kulkarni,(2017),APRIMERONFINITEELEMENTANALYSIS,LaxmiPublications,First edition.

RandyShih,*(2016),IntroductiontoFiniteElementAnalysisUsingSOLIDWORKSSimulation,* SDCPublications.

A.JDaviesRao S.S.,(2017),*TheFiniteElementMethodwithAnIntroductionPartial Differential Equations* byOxford,Second edition.

SalomeMeca,SyllignakisStefanos,PetrVosynek,,(2018),FiniteElementAnalysis,Aster KindleEdition,AmazonDigitalServicesLLC.

MaryKathrynThompson,JohnMartinThompson,Butterworth-Heinemann;(2017),*ANSYS andMatlab©MechanicalAPDLforFiniteElementAnalysis,*KindleEdition,1edition.

Epilogue

I hope , it was a nice reading of all these important two marks...

It will be of good importance to again mention that, this book is intended to provide the readers, especially the students community with enriched knowledge on the 2 marks questions and answers of Finite Element Methods. This subject normally appears in the seventh semester of B.E or B.Tech (Mechanical Engineering) course. Students will definitely find this small book very useful not only for their studies but also for their placement opportunities, where nowadays lots of technical questions are expected from problem oriented subjects like Finite Element Methods.

All the Best...

****

(In addition to the above questions, students can prepare all the important formulae also like Stiffness matrix, Shape functions in all units. Thanks)

****